It's  ir

It's Not Fair

V. Gilbert Beers

Illustrated by Tonda Rae Nalle

VICTOR BOOKS

A DIVISION OF SCRIPTURE PRESS PUBLICATIONS INC.
USA CANADA ENGLAND

Published in Wheaton, Illinois by Victor Books/SP Publications, Inc., Wheaton, Illinois.

ISBN 1-56476-312-9

Printed in the United States of America
1 2 3 4 5 6 7 8 9 10 - 98 97 96 95 94

TO PARENTS AND TEACHERS

What does your child do when a problem comes along? How does she respond to it? Where does he find the solution?

What we need is a good role model—someone who faces problems as we do, but knows the right way to resolve them. The Muffin Family is a role-model family. They face problems much like the ones that bother us daily. But there's a difference. The Muffins are not quite like their neighbors. You will soon learn that they are Christians, and thus they meet their problems with Bible truth.

The Muffins aren't perfect. Neither are you and I. But they are Christian. They aren't free from problems. But they resolve them—God's Way.

If you're looking for a book that will role-model Bible truth at work in a family much like yours, meet The Muffin Family.

V. Gilbert Beers

"It's not fair," Maxi complained. "Why do I have to feed Ruff and Tuff this morning?

It's Mini's turn to feed our dog and cat. Why did she have to get sick?"

Before Mommi and Poppi could answer Maxi,
they heard Mini grumbling in her bedroom.

"It's not fair," said Mini. "I have to lie here in bed sick while Maxi gets to play with Ruff and Tuff. It's just not fair."

Mommi looked at Poppi.
Poppi looked at Mommi.
Mommi and Poppi looked at each other. Then they decided to change the subject.

"Would you like to help us pull weeds in the flower bed after breakfast?" Poppi asked Maxi. "It's a family project, you know."

"Will Mini help too?" Maxi asked.

"Not when she's sick in bed," said Poppi.

"But that's not fair," said Maxi.

"Mini lies around while I'm out there working."

Maxi had just finished saying that when Mini called from her room. "Mommi, do I have to stay in bed all day?"

"Yes, Mini," Mommi answered.

"What's Maxi going to do?"

"He's going to help us in the flower bed."

"But that's not fair," said Mini.
"I have to lie here in this old bed
while Maxi goes outside."

13

Mommi and Poppi decided there wasn't a good answer at the moment, so they would talk later about "it's not fair."

That evening Mini was propped up at the dinner table while Maxi slouched in his chair. Both were thinking about how things were "just not fair."

Maxi didn't say a word. Neither did Mini.

"Well, if nobody wants to talk while we eat, I think I'll read a magazine," said Mommi.

"Me too," said Poppi.

Maxi and Mini looked surprised. Mommi and Poppi never read at the table except to read something to the whole family.

"Look at this beautiful lady," said Mommi, pointing to a picture on the magazine cover. "Why can't I be beautiful like that? It's just not fair!"

"But…but…" Mini stammered. She didn't have a good answer.

"Look at this beautiful house," said Poppi, pointing to a picture on the front cover of his magazine. "I always wanted a house like that, but I could never afford it. Why does this fellow have one? It just isn't fair!"

"But…but…" Maxi stammered. He didn't have a good answer either.

19

"Well?" Mommi asked. "Is it fair that I'm not as beautiful as she?"

"And is it fair that I don't have a house as nice as this?" asked Poppi.

Maxi and Mini stared at each other.
What should they say?

"But Mommi, I love you just the way you are," said Mini. "If you looked like her, you wouldn't look like my wonderful Mommi."

"And I love my house just the way it is," said Maxi. "I wouldn't trade our house for that house."

"That's nice," said Poppi. "But is it fair when one person has more than another? Is it fair for someone to be better looking,

or have a nicer home
or have better clothes
or more money?"

Maxi and Mini looked at each other. "No, it isn't fair," said Mini. "But maybe there's something more important than having everything exactly fair."

"Like what?" asked Mommi

"Like being grateful for what you do have," said Maxi.

"Especially if you can't do anything about it, and you know that's what God gave you," said Mini.

"You mean you wouldn't trade Mommi for that beautiful lady?" Poppi asked.

"NO!" shouted Maxi and Mini.

"I wouldn't either," said Poppi, giving Mommi a big hug. "So Mommi has something very special. She has a family that loves her just the way she is."

"And you don't have to get that old house either," said Maxi. "We love our house just as it is."

"And our Poppi," said Mini.

"And our Ruff and Tuff," said Maxi. "I'll even feed them tonight, and that's fair!"